EXPLORERS DISCOVERING THE WORLD

THE EXPLORATION OF

ARABIA AND ASIA

Tim Cooke

Gareth Stevens
Publishing

Please visit our website, www.garethstevens.com. For a free color catalog of all our high-quality books, call toll-free 1-800-542-2595 or fax 1-877-542-2596.

Library of Congress Cataloging-in-Publication Data

Cooke, Tim, 1961-
 The exploration of Arabia and Asia / Tim Cooke.
    p. cm. — (Explorers discovering the world)
 Includes index.
ISBN 978-1-4339-8616-1 (pbk.)
ISBN 978-1-4339-8617-8 (6-pack)
ISBN 978-1-4339-8615-4 (library binding)
1. Asia—Discovery and exploration—Juvenile literature. 2. Arabian Peninsula—Discovery and explora-
tion—Juvenile literature. 3. Explorers—Asia—Biography—Juvenile literature. 4. Explorers—Arabian
Peninsula—Biography—Juvenile literature. I. Title.
 DS5.95.C66 2013
 915—dc23

2012037842

ISBN 978-1-4339-8616-1 (pbk.)
ISBN 978-1-4339-8617-8 (6-pack)
ISBN 978-1-4339-8615-4 (library binding)

Published in 2013 by
Gareth Stevens Publishing
111 East 14th Street, Suite 349
New York, NY 10003

For Brown Bear Books Ltd:
Editorial Director: Lindsey Lowe
Managing Editor: Tim Cooke
Children's Publisher: Anne O'Daly
Art Director: Jeni Child
Designer: Lynne Lennon
Picture Manager: Sophie Mortimer

Picture Credits
Front Cover: Shutterstock: main: **Thinkstock:** Photos.com inset.

Corbis: The Gallery Collection 32; **Library of Congress:** 38; **Public Domain:** 11b, 21b, 24, 29, 30, 39, 43t,
National Palace Museum in Taipei 18t, Private Collection 41; **Robert Hunt Library:** 44; **Shutterstock:** 6, 18b,
33t, 33b, 35, Antonio Abrignani 13tr, 36, Paulo Afonos 26, George Nazmi Bebawi 15, Ron Frank 21t, Jakrit
Kiraratwaro 42, Stephen Aaron Rees 23, Valery Shanin 9, Konstantin Shishkin 14, David Steele 11t, Stefano
Tronci 17; **Thinkstock:** AbleStock 45t, Design Pics 27, Hemera 7, 8, 22, 25, 34, 37, istockphoto 5t, 5b, 10, 31b,
40, Photos.com 31t, Top Photo Group 28; **Topfoto:** Fortean 45b, Roger-Viollet 12.

Brown Bear Books has made every attempt to contact the copyright holders. If anyone has any information
please contact smortimer@windmillbooks.co.uk

Manufactured in the United States of America
1 2 3 4 5 6 7 8 9 12 11 10

CPSIA compliance information: Batch #CW13GS: For further information contact Gareth Stevens, New York,
New York at 1-800-542-2595.

CONTENTS

INTRODUCTION

Travel across Asia began early. The Silk Road—in fact a network of trade routes—linked the civilizations of China, south Asia, and west Asia. Many of the first explorers were merchants. Others were pilgrims, such as the Chinese Buddhist monks who visited sites in India linked with the Buddha.

From the seventh century A.D., the Muslims of Arabia established an empire that stretched from North Africa deep into central Asia. That encouraged Muslim travelers to explore the areas under Islamic control.

European Attitudes

European exploration in Asia was led by missionaries seeking to make converts. Later, Asia became the scene of colonial conflict as European powers sought to carve out empires. The French, British, and Russians established their influence in the region, bringing eager explorers and mapmakers. Arabia meanwhile was seen as exotic and mysterious: it drew a series of notable explorers—female as well as male—who often traveled in disguise to avoid official travel restrictions.

The closed Himalayan kingdom of Tibet, with its Buddhist monasteries hidden in the mountains, attracted many explorers in the 18th and 19th centuries.

Nomads from the plains of central Asia built the Mongol Empire, which stretched across the continent from China in the east to the Black Sea in the west.

128 B.C–1433

CHINESE EXPLORERS

China was united as a single country in 221 B.C. under its first emperor, Qin Shi Huang. He built a 3,000-mile (4,800-km) wall along the border to keep out invaders, isolating the empire. But in 128 B.C., Emperor Wu of the Han dynasty allowed his ambassador, Chang Ch'ien, to travel outside the empire.

This statue of Admiral Zheng He stands in Malaysia; Zheng He led China's voyages of exploration in the early 15th century.

The Chinese built the Great Wall to keep out nomadic peoples from the northwest—but it also discouraged the Chinese themselves from heading west.

Chang Ch'ien was the first Chinese explorer. He headed to what is now Afghanistan to make an alliance with the Bactrians against the Xiongnu, who raided China and Bactria. But he was captured by the Xiongnu and kept as a slave for 10 years.

The Silk Road

After he was freed, Chang Ch'ien was sent on a second mission in 115 B.C. This time he traveled widely in central Asia. He reported back to the emperor about the peoples he found. He also opened routes for Chinese traders. The routes were the basis of what became known as the Silk Road.

DID YOU KNOW?

The famous Roman poet Virgil thought that Chinese silk grew on trees. He did not know about silkworms.

THE SILK ROAD

The Silk Road was the land route between China and Europe. In fact, there was more than one road, and it carried more than silk. Porcelain and spices also headed west, while luxuries such as glass and scented woods were taken to China, along with ideas such as Buddhism. Caravans used the routes through central Asia. Few traders traveled the whole route: they went part way, then sold their goods on.

A Chinese junk sails in Hong Kong harbor; junks were sturdy and could carry large amounts of cargo, making them ideal vessels for trade.

The next Chinese explorers were Buddhist monks. They wanted to visit shrines in India, where Buddhism had begun in the sixth century B.C. Monks such as Fa Hsien and Hsuan-Tsang traveled through central Asia. They wrote accounts of their journeys.

Sea Travel

Later pilgrims also traveled from China to India by sea. They sailed on foreign merchant ships that were involved in the spice trade. By the

12th century, the Chinese controlled the eastern end of the spice trade. But they did not think it was worth exploring new lands. They thought other cultures were inferior.

Looking Outward

In the 15th century, the Ming Dynasty sent Admiral Zheng He to explore the Indian Ocean. He reported that China did indeed have little to learn from the outside world.

ZHENG HE

Between 1405 and 1433, Admiral Zheng He made seven voyages in the Indian Ocean. His fleet of more than 300 vessels visited southeast Asia, south Asia, the Middle East, and the east coast of Africa. The expedition gave out gifts intended to show the superiority of Chinese culture.

These Buddhist monuments stand on the Silk Road where it enters China, at Dunhuang; Buddhists were some of China's earliest explorers.

ARABIAN EXPLORERS

In the seventh century A.D., the Arabs conquered a huge area from Spain in the west to India in the east. They were spreading their Islamic religion. The Arabs came from the desert. They preferred to travel overland in caravans. Later, however, they also became expert sea travelers.

Muslim pilgrims surround the Kaaba in Mecca; the Islamic duty to visit Mecca encouraged early Muslim explorers.

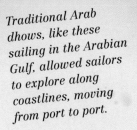

Traditional Arab dhows, like these sailing in the Arabian Gulf, allowed sailors to explore along coastlines, moving from port to port.

DID YOU KNOW?

One of the first Arab explorers was a merchant named Suleyman. He wrote his *Relation of India and China* in A.D. 751.

AL-IDRISI

The Muslim geographer al-Idrisi traveled widely throughout Europe and Africa in the 12th century. King Roger II of Sicily commissioned al-Idrisi to draw maps for him of all the parts of the world that were then known. In 1154, al-Idrisi produced the Book of Roger, *with 70 maps. The work summarized everything Arab geographers then knew about the world.*

Early Arab explorers included Ibn Fadlan. He traveled overland in A.D. 921 to the Volga River in Russia. Another explorer, al-Masudi, traveled as far as India, China, and east Africa.

Muslim Travelers

Ibn Hauqal was another 10th-century traveler. He spent more than 25 years journeying around the Muslim empire. He reached the heart of Africa and the island of Sicily in the Mediterranean Sea.

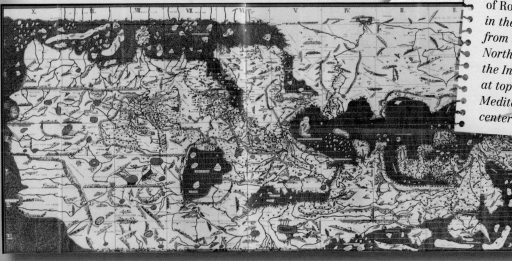

This map from the Book of Roger *is oriented in the opposite way from modern maps. North is at the bottom, the Indian Ocean is at top left, and the Mediterranean is in the center right.*

1325–1354

IBN BATTUTA

The Moroccan Ibn Battuta traveled across the Muslim world and beyond. He earned a living wherever he went by practicing Islamic law. In 1325, Ibn Battuta left his birthplace of Tangier for Tunis. From there, he set off on a pilgrimage to the holy city of Mecca.

With a guide, Ibn Battuta (right) visits ancient ruins in Egypt during his travels in this engraving from the 19th century.

DID YOU KNOW?

Ibn Battuta's travels could be dangerous. He almost drowned in a storm on the Black Sea; he was also attacked by pirates.

At Alexandria in Egypt, Ibn Battuta met a famous Islamic sufi, or teacher, who urged him to travel to meet other sufis in east Asia.

Pilgrims pray at the Kaaba, the shrine at Mecca. Ibn Battuta's first journey was the pilgrimage to Mecca that all Muslims hope to make at least once.

Ibn Battuta crossed northern Africa. He joined a caravan for added safety. At Alexandria in Egypt, he met a Muslim teacher who urged him to visit holy men in India and China.

Mecca and Beyond

Ibn Battuta eventually reached Arabia via Syria. He visited the holy cities of Mecca and Medina, then set off for Baghdad and Tabriz. In 1328, he sailed for east Africa, visiting Arab settlements on the coast.

DICTIONARY OF COUNTRIES

Yaqut al-Hamawi was the greatest geographer of the 13th century, despite his humble beginnings. He was sold as a slave, but his owner later freed him. Yaqut learned to read and write. His skills allowed him to work as he traveled around the Muslim empire. He recorded everything he learned in the Dictionary of Countries, an encyclopedia full of geographical facts about the Muslim world.

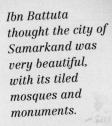

1325-1354

Ibn Battuta thought the city of Samarkand was very beautiful, with its tiled mosques and monuments.

Back in Mecca in 1330, Ibn Battuta embarked on his longest trip. He set off overland to India via Asia Minor (Turkey). On the way, he visited the great Christian capital of Constantinople and sailed across the Black Sea.

The Heart of Asia

Most of Asia was ruled by the Mongols. They had converted to Islam and welcomed the traveler. Ibn Battuta visited cities along the Silk Road, such as Samarkand. In India, he worked as a judge in Delhi before traveling to Sri Lanka and the Maldives. He reached China in 1345, where he saw porcelain and paper money for the first time. The following year, he set out for home—but not by the most direct route.

DID YOU KNOW?

In all, Ibn Battuta's travels took him 75,000 miles (120,000 km) throughout Asia and North Africa.

Indirect Journey

On his way home, Ibn Battuta visited the Islamic kingdom of Granada in Spain and crossed to Africa. He visited the fabled city of Timbuktu and sailed down what he thought was the Nile River; it was actually the Niger.

When Ibn Battuta got home, he dictated an account of all he had seen—and produced a remarkable record of the Islamic world in the 14th century.

LEO AFRICANUS

One of the great Muslim travelers after Ibn Battuta was Leo Africanus. He was born Muhammad al-Fasi in Granada, Spain, in about 1485. He traveled south of the Sahara in Africa. He later converted to Christianity and took the name Johannes Leo. He wrote a book about his African travels. It earned him the nickname Leo Africanus.

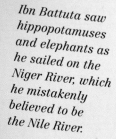

Ibn Battuta saw hippopotamuses and elephants as he sailed on the Niger River, which he mistakenly believed to be the Nile River.

MARCO POLO

This 14th-century painting depicts the three Polos (center, right) about to board a boat in Venice to begin their journey to east Asia in 1271.

Marco Polo's book about his travels shaped European views of Asia for centuries. The Polo family were traders in Venice. In 1266, Marco's father and uncle, the brothers Niccolò and Maffeo Polo, had traveled to China and met Kublai Khan, the Mongol ruler. They brought back letters from Kublai to the pope in Rome.

Kublai Khan asked the pope to send 100 European thinkers to his capital, Beijing, to debate ideas. Instead, Niccolò and Maffeo Polo set off back to China in 1271 with just two Christian monks—and young Marco.

Back to China

The party soon entered a war zone. The monks decided to go home. The three Polos carried on. They followed the Silk Road through Armenia, Persia, and Afghanistan, and over the Pamir Mountains to China.

DID YOU KNOW?

When Niccolò and Maffeo Polo arrived in Beijing it was a brand new city, built by Kublai as his new capital.

The Polos' route along the Silk Road crossed many deserts and mountains, like the high Pamir Mountains between Afghanistan and Tajikistan.

KUBLAI KHAN

Kublai belonged to the Mongol dynasty started by his grandfather, the fearsome Genghis Khan. Kublai became great khan in about 1259. After conquering China in 1279, he broke with the Mongols' nomadic lifestyle and built Beijing as a permanent capital. Kublai was a Buddhist but was tolerant of other religions. With no political tradition to follow, Kublai was happy to employ foreigners like the Polos in his court.

Kublai was pleased to see Niccolò and Maffeo. Marco became a favorite of the khan, who sent him on special diplomatic journeys to many parts of China, as well as to Burma and India. The Polos didn't leave until 17 years later. They accompanied a Mongol princess on a voyage to Persia, then returned to Venice in 1295.

Marco's Account

The travels of the Polos might have been forgotten. But after he returned home, Marco was taken prisoner by rival traders from the city of Genoa. During a year in jail, he dictated his stories to another prisoner.

This contemporary miniature shows Kublai Khan (top, on black horse) hunting with members of his court.

The Mongols from the plains of central Asia built an empire that stretched across the continent; their descendants still live traditional nomadic lives on the plains.

The Silk Road was home to wealthy cities such as Samarkand and Bukhara, but also to modest settlements like this village in a valley in Pakistan.

An Early Bestseller

Marco's book, called *Il Milione*, was a huge hit. It described "the marvels of the world," like Zanzibar and Japan (Cipangu). European readers were fascinated by his tales of the Mongol empire, the wealth of China (Cathay), and what he saw in India. But was it true? Many scholars think Marco included things he could not have not seen himself but had learned about from others.

DID YOU KNOW?

Kublai's grandfather, Genghis Khan, began the Mongol conquest of China. Kublai made China a powerful empire.

THE CATALAN ATLAS

The Jewish mapmaker Abraham Cresques worked for the king of Aragon. In 1375, he created the Catalan Atlas, with maps based on the accounts of travelers, including the Polos. It had lots of useful facts, such as accurate distances and directions. Unlike other maps, it did not try to fill in gaps with imaginary details.

FERDINAND MAGELLAN

The Portuguese noble Ferdinand Magellan made two errors when he sailed for the Spice Islands in Asia. The errors led him to become the first man to sail around the world. He set off in 1519 believing the Pacific Ocean was much smaller than it is. He also thought the Spice Islands lay off South America.

Mountains rise over a lake in Patagonia. Magellan's decision to spend the winter in Patagonia sparked a mutiny among his crew.

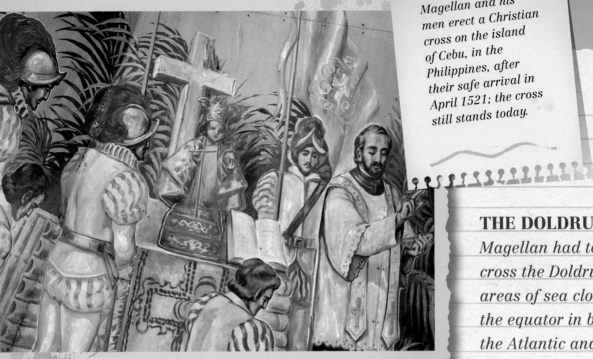

Magellan and his men erect a Christian cross on the island of Cebu, in the Philippines, after their safe arrival in April 1521; the cross still stands today.

THE DOLDRUMS

Magellan had to cross the Doldrums, areas of sea close to the equator in both the Atlantic and the Pacific Oceans. The Doldrums mark where the northern and southern trade winds meet. The results are unpredictable. Sometimes the sea can be so calm sailing ships can't move; at other times, huge storms rage. Sailors never know what to expect.

Magellan had been on the first Portuguese expedition to the Spice Islands—now part of Indonesia—in 1511. Back in Europe, he moved to Spain and put together his own expedition.

A Mutinous Crew

The Spanish king, Charles V, funded the expedition. That gave a lot of influence to a powerful bishop, Juan Fonseca, who made sure his relatives and friends were on the expedition, including three of the ships' captains. That would have serious consequences for Magellan.

Of Magellan's original five ships, two were abandoned, one was taken by mutineers, and another was seized by the Portuguese.

DID YOU KNOW?

Juan Fonseca's friends on the expedition caused constant trouble for Magellan and led at least two mutinies.

In the Philippines, Magellan became caught up in local wars; it was while fighting for the sultan of Cebu that he was killed defending his men.

Magellan intended to reach the Spice Islands by sailing west. He hoped to sail down the South American coast and find a strait linking the Atlantic and the Pacific Oceans.

The Doldrums

Fonseca's three captains caused many problems. They challenged Magellan's authority, and Magellan repeatedly put them under arrest. Finally, they seized three ships. Magellan put down the mutiny and executed one of the captains. The expedition spent the winter in Patagonia. After another mutiny, mutineers sailed one ship back to Spain. But Magellan found the strait in October 1520.

An Untimely End

Magellan set course across the Pacific. Failing to make landfall, the fleet had no fresh water or food for two months. Magellan finally reached the Philippines, but he died there in a fight with local warriors in April 1521.

The two remaining ships sailed to the Spice Islands. The *Victoria*, under Juan del Cano, reached Spain on September 6, 1522. The *Trinidad* was seized by the Portuguese; its crew reached home years later.

DID YOU KNOW?

Only one of Magellan's five ships—the *Victoria*—made it back to Spain. There were just 18 men on board.

Francis Drake sailed into the Pacific in 1578 to plunder Spanish colonies there. He returned to England two years later.

SIR FRANCIS DRAKE

The English privateer Francis Drake was the first sailor to take his own ship around the world. He sailed from Plymouth, England, on the Golden Hind *in December 1577. He aimed to attack Spanish colonies in Peru and treasure galleons off the coast. Drake sailed through the Strait of Magellan and up the coast. He looted Spanish ports as he went. He then sailed across the Pacific to the Spice Islands. From there, he rounded the Cape of Good Hope and returned to England.*

ANTHONY JENKINSON

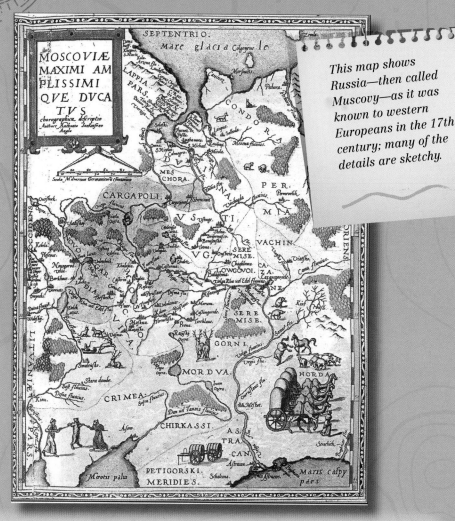

This map shows Russia—then called Muscovy—as it was known to western Europeans in the 17th century; many of the details are sketchy.

The English merchant Anthony Jenkinson was one of the first western Europeans to visit what is now Russia. He visited Moscow in 1557 on behalf of the Muscovy Company. The merchants of the company hoped to find an overland trade route to China.

In Moscow, Jenkinson met the czar, Ivan the Terrible. He then sailed down the Volga River and east across the Caspian Sea to Muslim-controlled Turkistan. In 1558, he reached Bukhara, an ancient Muslim trading town on the Silk Road.

Persia, Not China

Jenkinson returned to England with a new idea. The Muscovy Company should trade with Persia instead of China. He traveled to Persia in 1561, but found that the Persian shah had no wish to trade with Christians. Jenkinson's second trip to central Asia was therefore his last.

Bukhara stood on the Silk Road in what is now Uzbekistan. The city's great wealth convinced Jenkinson that trade with Persia could be very profitable for the English.

RICHARD CHANCELLOR

Another Englishman had met Ivan the Terrible in Moscow before Jenkinson. In 1553, Richard Chancellor and another explorer, Hugh Willoughby, sailed to northern Russia to find the Northeast Passage to Asia. They split up. Chancellor sailed into the White Sea and landed on the coast. When Ivan heard of his arrival, he invited him to Moscow, where Chancellor established trading relations with Ivan's lands.

1582–1716

JESUITS IN ASIA

The Jesuits were monks of the Society of Jesus, which aimed to spread the Catholic faith across the world. Their dedication meant they were often more successful than European traders in reaching remote places. Early Jesuit accounts became important sources of geographical information about China and east Asia.

This statue of Matteo Ricci stands in Macau; Ricci was a skilled scholar who studied the Chinese language and the Confucian religion.

DID YOU KNOW?

Ricci drew a map of China that gave Europeans some of their first reliable information about the country.

Ricci was one of the first foreigners to live in Beijing and the first Westerner to enter the Forbidden City, the home of China's imperial government.

Around 1582, the Italian Jesuit Matteo Ricci set up a mission near Canton, a trading post in China. From there, he went to Beijing. Ricci impressed the emperor with decriptions of European technology. The emperor gave Ricci the rare privilege of living in Beijing.

Cathay or China?

Ricci had read about Marco Polo's account of his travels. He wondered if China was the Cathay that Polo had described. He thought it probably was. The Jesuit leaders sent more missionaries to try to find proof.

BENEDICT DE GOES

The Portuguese Jesuit de Goes was living in India when his superiors sent him to travel to China. De Goes left Agra in late 1603 and traveled across central Asia. Chinese officials delayed him at the border but allowed him to cross in November 1604. De Goes joined a caravan to Suzhou, from where he sent word to Ricci in Beijing. But by the time Ricci's messenger arrived in Suzhou in March 1607, de Goes had died.

1582—1716

The Potala Palace rises over Tibet's capital, Lhasa. Despite repeated visits, the Jesuits found it difficult to make converts in the mainly Buddhist country.

Various Jesuit explorers were sent overland from India to China. They included the Portuguese Benedict de Goes in 1604. Goes died while on his expedition, but he had proved that Cathay and China were the same.

Tibet and Beyond

The Jesuits went on to explore the more remote Himalayan areas. Antonio de Andrade traveled from India to Tsaparang in Tibet in 1624. Other Jesuits, Estevao Cacella and Joao Cabral, crossed the Himalayas into Tibet via Bhutan.

DID YOU KNOW?

For the six years he stayed in Lhasa, Father Ippolito Desideri was the only European in the tiny Tibetan capital.

In 1628, the Jesuits set up a mission in Shigatze. By 1635, it was abandoned. Tibet was a center of Buddhism; the people did not want to convert to Christianity.

Desideri and Freyre

Jesuits continued to visit Tibet. As late as 1716, Ippolito Desideri and Emmanuel Freyre reached Lhasa. Desideri stayed on in the city, studying Buddhist scriptures and writing about his experiences.

ANTONIO DE ANDRADE

Andrade was working in India when he heard about Christians living in Tibet. In early 1624, he joined Hindu pilgrims to travel across the snow-covered Himalayas before reaching Tsaparang in western Tibet. The king invited Andrade to return the next year and set up a Jesuit mission. Andrade accepted the invitation, but his mission ended when a revolution overthrew the king. The revolutionaries destroyed the church Andrade had built.

Jesuit travels in China and India enabled them to learn overland routes between the two great states via the Himalayan kingdoms of Tibet and Bhutan.

1552–1584

YERMAK TIMOFEEVICH

Yermak Timofeevich was a Cossack warrior who led the Russian conquest of Siberia. In 1552, Czar Ivan the Terrible defeated the khanate of Kazan. He wanted to expand Muscovy to the east, where there were valuable sources of fur. He asked the wealthy Strogonov family to lead the conquest of Siberia.

Despite their conquest, Yermak and his men found it difficult to feed themselves in Siberia and were at the mercy of raids by their Tatar enemies.

DID YOU KNOW?

Ivan hoped that Yermak would be able to conquer Siberia all the way to the Bering Strait in the far east.

Ivan the Terrible was famous for his cruelty, but his nickname didn't actually mean he was cruel; it meant he was awe inspiring.

In the 1570s, the Stroganovs hired Cossacks to conquer Siberia from its Tatar rulers. The Cossacks made Yermak their leader. In October 1582, Yermak and his 840 men defeated the Tatars at the Battle of Qashliq.

Continuing the Fight

Siberia became part of Muscovy, but the Tatars continued to raid Russian trade. Yermak tried to stop them. He died in a Tatar ambush in 1584.

SIBERIA

Siberia is a huge area of northern Asia that now belongs to Russia. Much of it lies within the Arctic Circle. Its vast rolling plains are covered in trees and marshes that stay frozen during the long winters. River valleys are the best routes through the harsh terrain. Some of the lowest temperatures ever recorded on Earth have been in Siberia.

Much of Siberia consists of tundra, where the soil remains frozen for most of the year and only evergreen trees, grasses, and mosses can grow.

VITUS BERING

Vitus Bering (right) and his deputy, Alexei Chirikov, prepare to explore the coast of Alaska in June 1741; Bering died on the voyage, but Chirikov returned safely.

The Danish-born navigator Vitus Bering was hired in 1725 by Czar Peter the Great of Russia. The czar wanted Bering to lead an expedition to set up trading links with China and India. Bering decided to build his own ship on the peninsula of Kamchatka in the Sea of Okhotsk, in far eastern Russia.

Kamchatka was so far east it took two years to reach and a further year to build the ship, the *St. Gabriel*. In 1728, Bering was finally ready to set sail.

Vitus Bering had already been sailing for eight years before he joined the fast-growing navy of Peter the Great in 1704.

The Bering Sea

Bering sailed north along the coast of Kamchatka and then into the sea that is now named for him. In August, Bering spotted an island, which he named St. Lawrence. He realized that this sea separated Asia and North America.

A fishing boat sails through the Bering Strait, the narrows in the north of the Bering Sea that separate Asia and North America.

PETER THE GREAT

Peter the Great is credited with creating modern Russia. He wanted to change his country from a backward, rural empire into one of Europe's great powers. He traveled across Europe in disguise in 1697 to learn what skills his people needed to begin to transform Russia. He brought in experts and encouraged the arts and sciences. Most Russians disliked his obsession with foreign ideas.

DID YOU KNOW?

Bering resigned from the Russian navy because his low rank embarrassed his wife; he rejoined after he was promoted.

1697–1741

With fall approaching, Bering turned the *St. Gabriel* back before the ship was trapped in the winter ice. The next spring, he set off again. With the winds against him, he sailed south to prove that Kamchatka was a peninsula. It was not joined to Japan, as some people suggested.

The Great Northern Expedition

The Russian senate was now eager to approve a three-part expedition. One part explored Russia's Arctic coast. A second part mapped the waters between Japan and Kamchatka. Bering was in charge of the third part, which explored the strait between Russia and North America.

The Kamchatka peninsula was so remote that many Russians believed it was joined to Japan until Bering proved otherwise.

Vitus Bering discovered the Aleutian chain of islands off Alaska on his first trip into the Bering Sea in 1728.

DID YOU KNOW?

The second ship in the expedition, under Alexei Chirikov, reached Alaska and returned safely to Petropavlovsk.

Bering set sail from Petropavlovsk in June 1741 with two ships. The other was commanded by the Russian explorer Alexei Chirikov. The ships became separated in a storm.

Alaska Sighted

At the end of July 1741, Bering saw Mount St. Elias in Alaska, but his progress north was blocked by thick fog. His return journey was slowed down by strong winds. In November 1741, he landed on an island east of Kamchatka for the winter, but he died there.

DISASTER OFF KAMCHATKA

On his return from Alaskan waters, Bering's expedition was slowed by strong winds. As fresh food ran out, many of the crew fell sick. Eventually, there weren't enough well men to sail the ship. They landed on an island, where they planned to spend the winter. But it was too late: around one-third of the men died from scurvy, including Bering.

1599–1910

ARABIA

Until about 1800, Europeans saw Arabia as a mysterious and mystical region of vast deserts and lush oases. The first known explorer was an English adventurer, Anthony Sherley, who crossed Arabia to reach Persia (Iran) in 1599. He wrote a long account of his adventures.

Many Western explorers in the desert adopted traditional ways of moving around, such as joining caravans traveling by camel.

DID YOU KNOW?

The Ottoman government would not issue permits to Westerners or protect them, making it hard to travel in Arabia.

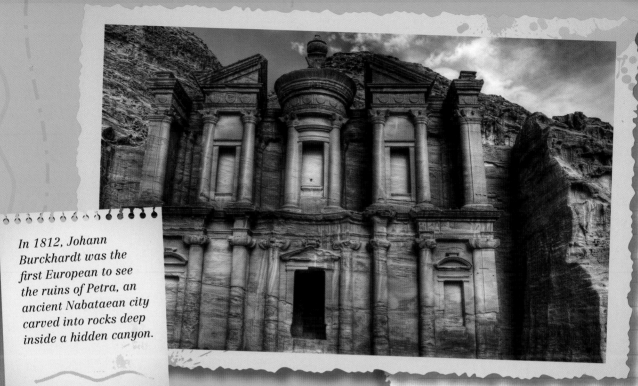

In 1812, Johann Burckhardt was the first European to see the ruins of Petra, an ancient Nabataean city carved into rocks deep inside a hidden canyon.

Under the Ottoman Empire, Western travel in Arabia was restricted. It was not until 1761 that the king of Denmark sponsored the first scientific exploration there. Only one of the six explorers who set out from Egypt survived.

An Arabian Fantasy

From the late 18th century, Europeans began to see Arabia as an exotic and romantic destination. As people grew richer, they started to visit the region's Roman ruins at Palmyra and Baalbek or the ancient cities of Damascus and Aleppo. One such traveler was the Swiss explorer Johann Burckhardt.

JOHANN BURCKHARDT

Burckhardt set out for Africa but instead went to Arabia. He disguised himself as an Arab or a Turk to move around easily. He saw the ruins of Palmyra, Baalbek, and Petra. He also got permission to visit the holy cities of Mecca and Medina. When he died in Cairo, he was honored with a Muslim tomb.

The Middle East also attracted military explorers. James Wellstead of the Royal Navy surveyed the Arabian coast in the 1830s, for example.

Traveling in Disguise

Many explorers traveled in disguise. The English scholar Richard Burton visited the holy cities of Medina and Mecca dressed as a Muslim. William Palgrave posed as a Christian Arab doctor in the 1860s in Persia, and Charles Doughty dressed as a Syrian merchant to travel.

The coastal ports of the Middle East had become a popular destination for wealthy Europeans by the early 1900s.

DID YOU KNOW?

Wilfred Thesiger crossed the world's largest sand desert, the Empty Quarter in Saudi Arabia, twice in the 1940s.

The Empty Quarter, or Rub al-Kahli, covers the southern part of the Arabian Peninsula; it is 250,000 square miles (650,000 sq km) of almost uninhabited desert.

Writers in Arabia

In 1888, Doughty wrote *Travels in Arabia Deserta* about his treks through the desert with Bedouin nomads. In 1910, Thomas Lawrence (Lawrence of Arabia) went to the Middle East and wrote about it in *Seven Pillars of Wisdom*. The endless deserts and their changing nature appealed to many writers and artists later in the 20th century, including Wilfred Thesiger and Freya Stark.

GERTRUDE BELL

Gertrude Bell was one of very few women travelers in west Asia. She visited Persia in 1892 and learned to speak Farsi. In 1899, she moved to Damascus to study Arabic and decided to explore the region. It was dangerous for women to travel alone, but she did just that. Bell eventually settled in Damascus. She earned the nickname "the uncrowned queen of Iraq."

1806-1882

MAPPING INDIA

In the mid-19th century, the British set out to map their vast Indian colony using local recruits. The workers traveled in disguise to avoid hostility from locals who resented British rule. They secretly recorded their information. They were known as "pundits," meaning "wise men."

DID YOU KNOW?

The British began mapping India in 1806. They expected the work to take five years; instead, it took over 60 years.

Mount Everest was surveyed by the British and named for an early director of the Great Trigonometrical Survey, Colonel Sir George Everest.

British army engineers like Colonel Thomas Tupper Carter-Campbell helped survey India by working for the Great Trigonometrical Survey in the 1860s.

KISHEN SINGH

Working under the code name "A.K.," Kishen Singh was the most remarkable of all the pundits. In 1878, he started a 3,000-mile (4,800 km) journey from India to Lhasa and on to Dunhuang, where the Silk Route entered China, and then back home again. Over the course of his journey, Singh was robbed, arrested, and sent to jail. By the time he got back to India in 1882, everyone had given him up for dead. But he presented his report to the British authorities. It helped them to fill in missing information about Tibet.

The pundits walked thousands of miles. They used Buddhist rosary beads to record their steps. They hid their notes and compasses inside Buddhist prayer wheels. The men were trained to memorize what they had seen for months at a time.

Pundit Number 1

Nain Singh—code name "Number 1"— traveled from Katmandu to Lhasa, in Tibet. He traveled through Tibet and traced the source of the Brahmaputra River. By the time he returned to India, he had covered 1,250 miles (2,000 km) in 2.5 million steps.

THE FRENCH IN INDOCHINA

The Khong Falls on the Mekong River are not very tall, but the speed of the water prevents ships from sailing past them.

The French had been involved in Indochina— modern Vietnam, Cambodia, and Laos—for many years. Ernest Doudart de Lagrée became French ambassador to the Cambodian king in 1863. He traveled around Cambodia, visiting the newly discovered ruins of Angkor and the Mekong River.

When Mouhot discovered the ruins of Angkor, they were lost in the jungle; even locals had forgotten why the city had been built or by whom.

In 1866, Doudart de Lagrée led an expedition to discover if the Mekong was navigable. Many of the explorers fell sick. But they soon confirmed that the Mekong could not be navigated to the ocean.

The Mighty Mekong

After Doudart de Lagrée died of dysentery, his deputy, Marie-Joseph-François Garnier, continued to map the Mekong into China. He mapped about 3,100 miles (5,000 km) of the river. When he returned to Paris in 1868, people thought he was exaggerating.

ANGKOR

Angkor in Cambodia was the capital of the Khmer dynasty from the 9th to the 13th centuries. Khmer rulers built spectacular Buddhist and Hindu temples there. After the city was abandoned in 1431, the jungle took over. Angkor lay forgotten until the French explorer Henri Mouhot accidentally discovered it in 1860.

The vast Hindu temple of Angkor Wat is one of the largest of the stone monuments at Angkor. Its five towers are modeled on the shape of lotus flowers.

1870–1935

CENTRAL ASIA

By 1870, much of central Asia had not been mapped. European explorers saw it as a last frontier. It had the highest mountains in the world. The great rivers of Asia had their sources there. Most mysterious was the Buddhist kingdom of Tibet. Britain and Russia both wanted to control the region.

Sven Hedin failed to reach Lhasa in Tibet, but on four expeditions in central and east Asia between 1893 and 1935, he did successfully make many important geographical discoveries.

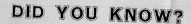

DID YOU KNOW?

"Lhasa" means "holy place" in Tibetan. Buddhists saw the city as holy because it was the home of the Dalai Lama.

The Potala Palace in Lhasa was home to the Tibetans' traditional spiritual leader and king, the Dalai Lama, who led Tibetan Buddhism.

The Russian explorer Nikolai Mikhailovich Przhevalski led four expeditions in the region from 1870 to 1885. He covered over 20,000 miles (32,000 km) and made important botanical, zoological, and geographical discoveries. His British equivalent was the little-known Ney Elias, who made eight major expeditions.

Roof of the World

In 1891, British missionary Annie Taylor made a 1,300-mile (2,000 km) journey to try to get into the Tibetan capital, Lhasa. She failed. The Swedish explorer Sven Hedin disguised himself as a monk to enter Lhasa in 1901 but was sent away.

WOMAN IN LHASA

Alexandra David Néel was a French-Belgian explorer. She was an expert on Buddhism and had met the Dalai Lama. Lhasa was forbidden to foreigners, but in 1924, Néel got into Lhasa disguised as a monk after a four-month walk. She lived in the Tibetan capital for two months.

Alexandra David Néel was one of only a few Europeans—and even fewer women—who managed to sneak into the Tibetan capital in Lhasa.

GLOSSARY

caravan A large group of pack animals and people traveling together.

colony A settlement founded in a new territory by people from another country.

continent A very large landmass.

Cossack A member of a warlike people from southern Russia.

Dalai Lama The spiritual leader of Tibetan Buddhists.

dhow A traditional Arab sailing vessel with triangular sails.

expedition A journey made for a particular purpose.

Great Trigonometrical Survey A British mission to take accurate measurements of the landscape in India.

khanate An area ruled by a Mongol emperor known as a khan.

missionary A person who preaches in order to persuade other people to convert to a religion.

Muslim A follower of the Islamic religion.

mutiny An uprising by military or naval personnel against their commanders.

nomad Someone who has no permanent home but who moves around from season to season.

pilgrim A traveler who makes a journey, known as a pilgrimage, to visit a holy site.

privateer A pirate licensed by a government to raid other ships.

scurvy A disease caused by lack of vitamin C.

shah The title of the ruler of Persia.

survey To make scientific measurements of an area.

FURTHER INFORMATION

Books

Explorers: Great Tales of Adventure and Endurance. DK Publishing, 2010.

Feinstein, Stephen. *Marco Polo: Amazing Adventures in China* (Great Explorers of the World). Enslow Publishers, 2009.

Kramer, Sydelle. *Who Was Ferdinand Magellan?* Grosset and Dunlap, 2004.

Rumford, James. *The Traveling Man: The Journey of Ibn Battuta, 1325–1354*. Turtleback, 2004.

Senker, Cath. *Marco Polo's Travels on Asia's Silk Road* (Great Journeys Across Earth). Heinemann Educational Books, 2007.

Websites

http://www.silk-road.com/artl/marcopolo.shtml
Silk Road Foundation page about Marco Polo.

http://www.enchantedlearning.com/explorers/
Enchanted Learning timeline of explorers, including in Asia.

http://www.pbs.org/wgbh/nova/ancient/ancient-chinese-explorers.html
PBS/Nova pages about Admiral Zheng He.

http://www.bluesci.org/?p=2028
Cambridge University science magazine article about the Great Trigonometrical Survey in India.

INDEX